FIESTA!

TUNISIA

GROLIER

An Imprint of Scholastic Library Publishing
Danbury, Connecticut

Published for Grolier
an imprint of Scholastic Library Publishing
Old Sherman Turnpike, Danbury, Connecticut 06816
by Marshall Cavendish Editions
an imprint of Marshall Cavendish International
1 New Industrial Road, Singapore 536196

Set ISBN: 0-7172-5788-6
Volume ISBN: 0-7172-5804-1

Library of Congress Cataloging-in-Publication Data
Tunisia.
p. cm.—(Fiesta!)
Summary: Discusses the festivals and holidays of Tunisia and how the songs, food,
and traditions associated with these celebrations reflect the culture of the people.
1. Festivals—Tunisia—Juvenile literature. 2. Tunisia—Social life and customs—Juvenile literature.
[1. Festivals—Tunisia. 2. Holidays—Tunisia. 3. Tunisia—Social life and customs.]
I. Grolier (Firm). II. Fiesta! (Danbury, Conn.)
GT4889.T8T85   2004
394.26611—dc21   2003044854

For this volume
Author: Paul A. Rozario
Editor: Balvinder Sandhu
Designer: Geoslyn Lim
Production: Nor Sidah Haron
Crafts and Recipes produced by Stephen Russell

Printed by Everbest Printing Co. Ltd

Adult supervision advised for all crafts and recipes,
particularly those involving sharp instruments and heat.

CONTENTS

TUNISIA:

Tunisia is situated in North Africa and is bordered by the Mediterranean Sea to the north and northeast, Libya to the southeast, and Algeria in the west and southwest. The north of the country is mountainous, while southern Tunisia forms part of the Sahara Desert, the largest desert in the world.

▼ The **fennec** is a small fox found in the deserts of southern Tunisia. It has enormous ears and comes out only at night. During the day the fennec lives in tunnels that it has dug in the sand. The fennec is an endangered animal.

▲ An **oasis** is a place in the desert where plants can grow because of the water that has collected there. Date palms grow in oases, and these palms produce dates, a sweet, sticky fruit that Tunisians love to eat. The largest desert oasis in Tunisia is Douz, which supports about 400,000 date palms!

Carthage

Cap Bon Peninsula

El Haouaria

TUNIS

Dougga

MEDITERRANEAN
SEA

El-Jem

Djerba Island

Douz

Ksour Ouled Soltane

ALGERIA

LIBYA

▲ **Tunis** is the capital city of Tunisia. The medina, or old town, is the oldest part of Tunis, and you can see many beautiful examples of Islamic architecture there. You can also explore the many suks, or markets, that are found in the medina. These suks sell anything from carpets to birdcages.

◀ The **Roman amphitheater** at El-Jem in central Tunisia is one of the best-preserved ancient Roman buildings in Africa. It is also the largest Roman structure in Africa. The amphitheater was built around A.D. 230 and can seat 30,000 people.

RELIGIONS

The main religion in Tunisia is Islam, while the remaining minority of the population are Christians, Jews, and some who do not follow any religion.

TUNISIA is an Islamic country, with nearly 90 percent of the population practicing the Islamic religion. In the 7th century A.D. the Prophet Muhammad spread the message of Islam.

Followers of Islam are called Muslims, and their holy scriptures are contained in a book called the Koran. Muslims are also guided by the example of the Prophet Muhammad's life, which has been written in a series of texts called *hadith*. Islam teaches that there is only one God, called Allah, and that Muhammad is his prophet. It also teaches that the God of Judaism and Christianity is the same as Allah. Parts of the Bible and the Torah are similar to the Koran, and many figures such as Abraham and Jesus appear in the Koran.

There are five rules in Islam. First, Muslims must believe that there is only one God and that Muhammad is his prophet. Second, Muslims must pray five times a day, facing Mecca in Saudi Arabia, the holiest city of Islam. Third, Muslims must help the poor by giving donations. Fourth, Muslims must fast during the holy month of Ramadan.

Finally, Muslims who can afford to should make a pilgrimage, or *Hajj*, to Mecca at least once in their lifetimes.

Tunisia's Muslims celebrate mainly Aid el-Fitr (known as Aid es-Seghir in Tunisia)

Followers of Islam must pray five times a day, and that usually takes place at a mosque.

and Aid el-Adha (known as Aid el-Kebir in Tunisia).

The remaining people in Tunisia are Christians, Jews, and those who do not follow any religion. The Christian communities live mostly in the major cities, and their main festivals are Christmas and Easter.

Tunisia's island of Djerba is home to an ancient community of Jewish people. Tunisian Jews believe that the site of the El Griba synagogue on Djerba has been

When Muslims pray, they hold a bunch of prayer beads in their hands.

in use for more than 2,000 years. The actual buildings, however, were built in the 1920s.

GREETINGS FROM TUNISIA!

Arabic is the main language in Tunisia and has an alphabet of 28 consonants. Vowel sounds are shown by dots written above or below these consonants. The Arabic script is written from right to left. French is also spoken in Tunisia, particularly in the main cities. It is also used in business, higher education, and government. Many Tunisians also speak English and German. Another language spoken in Tunisia is the Berber language. There are many Berber languages and dialects, spoken by the few remaining Berber communities across North Africa.

How do you say...

Hello
Ass'lama

Welcome
Marhaba

How are you?
Labais?

Goodbye
Bisslama

Congratulations
Mabrouk

AID ES-SEGHIR

Aid es-Seghir is also called Aid el-Fitr, and it celebrates the end of the sacred month of Ramadan, during which Muslims fast from sunrise to sunset.

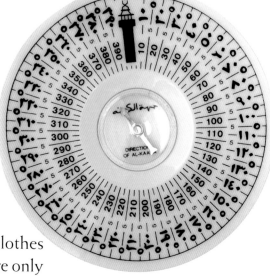

Muslims pray facing the direction of Mecca and use a compass such as this to locate where it is.

Families prepare for Aid es-Seghir during Ramadan. Women bake cakes made from dried fruits and almond paste, such as *baklawa*, *kaak*, and *makhroud*.

Families also make new clothes for the children, which are called *ahwayaj el Aid*, which means "clothes for Aid." Children are only allowed to wear them on the day of celebration.

This festival is a two-day holiday. Early in the morning on the first day children greet their parents with *"Aid Mabrouk,"* which is the traditional greeting for Aid. Children put on their new Aid clothes, and older members of the family are also dressed in their best.

Many Muslim households contain items with Arabic writing, such as this plate.

The mother of the family stays at home to receive visits from relatives and friends, while the father and children go to visit other relatives. They begin by visiting the grandparents, who do not go out. Then they visit close relatives, extended family, and finally, friends.

The children receive cakes and sweets at each house they visit. The adults also give the visiting children money as gifts, called *mahbat el Aid*.

At noon the whole family gathers at the home of the paternal grandfather for the sumptuous Aid es-Seghir meal. There is much food and many cakes to eat as dessert.

Later in the afternoon the children go to parks, accompanied by their parents. Here there are many stalls selling toys, firecrackers, and fireworks. The children use the money they have received to buy toys.

The children also spend some of their money at the photograph stands. These stands are covered with tapestries and pictures of Mecca, the city in Saudi Arabia that is the holiest city in Islam. These pictures are called *tasswirat el Aid*, or Aid photographs, and are usually taken with the whole family as a nice souvenir of the day.

Many people also go to the mosque early in the morning for Aid prayer, or *sallat el Aid*. Aid es-Seghir is also a celebration of forgiveness. It is a custom during this time for people to forgive their enemies and others who have wronged them. Family members can ask for pardon, or *smah*, from other members of the family to whom they have behaved badly.

On the second day of Aid, which is called *thany Aid*, people continue to make visits to homes. This time they visit people who are only distantly related. Those who were not able to visit on the first day of Aid can also go on the second day.

During the two days of Aid villages and towns are lit up with colored lights and flags, while streamers and banners hang from various buildings. Streets are congested with cars and people long into the night, and there is a festive atmosphere all around.

During Aid es-Seghir Muslims eat dates (left) and drink special drinks (right) made for the festival.

CHEOUDATH YITHRO

Tunisia is home to one of the most ancient communities of Jewish people. Most Tunisian Jews live on the island of Djerba, off the southern coast. Cheoudath Yithro is a festival celebrated by Tunisian Jews.

During the festival boys are served lots of food, and plates and cutlery are specially laid out for them.

Cheoudath Yithro is a Tunisian Jewish festival that remembers Jethro, the father-in-law of Moses. Moses led the Jews out of slavery from Egypt by parting the Red Sea so they could escape on dry land.

The story of Jethro tells about when he visited Moses after he had heard of the miraculous escape. Jethro was concerned that Moses was wearing himself out because of all the work he had to do as leader of the Jewish people.

Jethro suggested to Moses that he appoint people he trusted to help him with his work. Only the most difficult cases would be brought to his attention. This worked, and Moses was able to have more time for his family.

This story has special significance for Tunisian Jews. Following folklore, there was a time of a widespread epidemic of diphtheria, a disease that affects young children.

Also known as the "Festival of Boys," this day sees the boys of the house treated as kings.

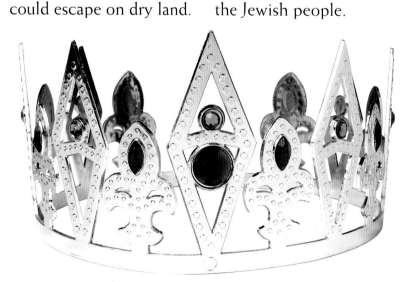

During this outbreak the community found that young boys were dying more than young girls. They prayed, and the epidemic finally stopped during the week they were reading the story of Jethro from the Jewish scriptures.

The families were so happy at this miracle that they made their boys kings for a day. That is why this day is also known as the "Festival of Boys."

The festival is held in the Jewish month of *shvat*, which is in January or February. A table is laid out complete with plates, glasses, forks, and spoons. A pigeon is cooked for each boy, as are pastries such as *yoyos* and *briks*.

Lots of attention is lavished on the boy-kings, as the family pampers them with food and drink. The atmosphere is very festive, and the story of Jethro is read out as families give thanks for the good health and safety of their children.

The Star of David is a popular symbol for the Jewish religion.

YOYOS

SERVES 4

2 eggs
3 tbsp sugar
3 tbsp oil (not olive oil)
1 tsp salt
2 tsp vanilla extract
2 tsp yeast
1 tsp cream of tartar
12 ozs flour

1 Beat the eggs and sugar in a large bowl. Add the oil bit by bit.

2 Add the yeast and other ingredients. Beat well.

3 Add the flour a little at a time, constantly beating the mixture.

4 Beat the mixture until it is the consistency of modeling clay. Let it stand for 45 minutes.

5 Roll out the dough into a sheet of about $1/2$ inch thickness.

6 Using doughnut cutters, cut out doughnuts from this sheet. Make sure there is a hole in the center of each doughnut.

7 Fry the doughnuts in cooking oil, 4 or 5 at a time. They should inflate. Fry until golden brown.

AID EL-KEBIR

Aid el-Kebir is also known as the Festival of Sacrifice. It follows the story from the Koran of the prophet Ibrahim. The festival is celebrated about nine weeks after Aid es-Seghir and lasts for two days.

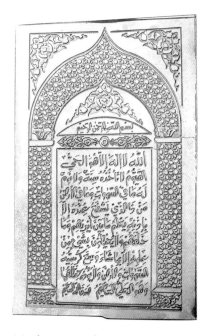

Muslims go to the mosque and say a special prayer on Aid el-Kebir.

The story of Aid el-Kebir comes from the Koran and tells how the prophet Ibrahim was asked by Allah to sacrifice his only son, Ismail.

Just as Ibrahim was raising his knife on his son, Allah replaced the boy with a ram, and Ismail was saved. Allah was so pleased with Ibrahim's obedience that He would not allow Ibrahim to sacrifice his son.

A main part of Aid el-Kebir involves the sacrifice of rams and sheep.

Families go to the markets a month before Aid el-Kebir to buy sheep and rams. At home the amimals are groomed, fed, and decorated with red ribbons. Patterns called *khomsa* (hand prints) are sometimes drawn in red dye on the animals' wool.

Children bring out their families' rams or sheep to a *houma*, which is usually a square, and they then decide whose animals are most beautiful.

They also organize tournaments in which the rams head-butt each other.

Adults sometimes bring their rams and join in too.

Families buy grills, barbecues, skewers, and charcoal, which will be used to roast the animals.

Two days before the festival the women buy ingredients that will be used to prepare the Aid meal. These dishes include couscous (a specialty made from semolina flour) and *osbanes* (a spicy dish made with the intestines and kidneys of sheep).

On the first day of Aid el-Kebir Tunisians go to the mosque early

in the morning to say the prayer for Aid, or the *sallat el Aid*. Children wake up with sad expressions, since this is the day the animals will be sacrificed.

In the streets there are cries of *"Dhabbah! Dhabbah!"* The *dhabbah* are people who slaughter the animals for a fee.

At 8:00 A.M. an incense lamp is lit, and the animals are prepared for the slaughter. They are tied up and faced in the direction of Mecca. Then they are killed, as special prayers are said. Some blood is taken to smear the walls of the house as a sign of blessing, or *baraka*. The mother of the family also makes a pattern on a wall with some blood. This pattern is called the Hand of Fatimah.

The women prepare the meat to be cooked. The entrails are made into *osbanes*, while couscous is cooked to go with the meat dishes. Meanwhile, the men prepare the meat for the barbecue.

By late morning the meat is roasting away. After the meal the family visits the grandparents to wish them *"Aid Mabrouk."*

On the second day any remaining meat from the day before is prepared in a dish called *kaddid*.

The women dry the meat in the sun for some days and put it in jars of oil to preserve it. The meat then lasts for several weeks. They also prepare *coscsy* *bilham*, which is couscous with meat. They put the food on a tray and take it to mosques, where it is distributed as a donation, or *sadaka*, to poor people who have gathered there.

By the end of Aid el-Kebir all the meat from the sacrificed animals has been used. Even the skins are cleaned and dried for use as carpets or blankets.

Tumeric powder (left) is popular in Tunisian dishes, and a meat barbecue (right) takes place on Aid el-Kebir.

TUNISIAN COUSCOUS

SERVES 4

4 lbs chopped lamb
4 large onions (finely chopped)
$^1/_2$ cup olive oil
6 ozs tomato paste
2 large tomatoes (chopped)
1 tbsp cumin
1 tsp black pepper
1 tsp curry powder
1 tsp cayenne pepper
5 garlic cloves

Salt to taste
2 medium bell peppers (chopped)
1 large butternut squash (mashed)
4 medium turnips (chopped)
4 medium carrots (chopped)
1 lb potatoes
2 cups dry couscous (cooked)
3 sprigs parsley (chopped)
2 medium lemons

1 Brown the lamb with the onions in a large pot.

2 Add tomato paste, and cook for 5 minutes, stirring frequently.

3 Add the tomatoes, spices, and bell peppers. Reduce flame to simmer.

4 Add the remaining vegetables and water to cover the mixture to within 3 inches of the top layer of vegetables.

5 Cook until meat and vegetables are tender.

6 Serve over the couscous, and garnish with parsley and lemons.

FESTIVAL OF THE KSOUR

Ksours *are secured Berber villages in southern Tunisia. They are architecturally unique because of* **ghorfas,** *which are rooms that have arched ceilings and are built on top of each other.*

Bottles of olive oil are among the items sold at the lively market during the festival.

The market in town also sells a selection of handmade jewelry.

The *ghorfa* is a room used to store grain. It faced a courtyard and was several stories high. As the *ksour* grew, more *ghorfas* would be added, and steps were sculpted into the sides to reach the *ghorfas* on the upper levels. Today many *ghorfas* have crumbled, but those that remain are used as homes.

The Festival of the Ksour takes place in one of the most famous and best preserved of the *ksours* – Ksour Ouled Soltane, where some of the *ghorfas* are a few hundred years old. The festival takes place in April, and the courtyards are used for musical performances.

Before the festival Berber tribesmen from all over Tunisia arrive in Ksour Ouled Soltane. They take part in the festival, which lasts for five days.

There are camel and horse races, as well as exhibitions of Berber life. There is also a lively market. Women display their woven fabrics and blankets, while others sell

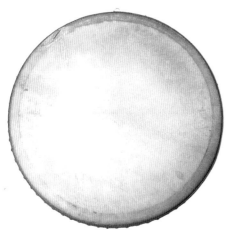

Musicians carry drums that accompany the dancers.

others, dates and olive oil. There are also many favorite local snacks, including *kab el-ghazal*, a delicious pastry horn filled with almond paste and honey. Other snacks to try are candied almonds, stuffed dates, and *makroud* – small cakes made from semolina and dates.

The performances in the courtyard at night are magical. The musicians, who play hand-held drums, tambourines, and trumpets, accompany the dancers. The performances last late into the night.

spices, food, baskets, and clothes. Some stalls sell brass lamps and pottery;

This clay model shows what a ksour looks like, with ghorfas atop one another.

ELLILLA EID

Ellila Eid Ellila Eid farha farha walomr jdid

Rabbi ittim Alayna Afrah hana

Wayajmaa shamlina sanaa wa sanaa

Fi lila zina ittim alhana illila illila illila Eid

A TALE OF TWO MICE

Larbi loved Leila, but Leila was always asking him to buy more beautiful objects.

She could never get enough fine jewelry and thick carpets. Poor Larbi!

ONCE UPON A TIME there was a mouse named Larbi who lived with his wife, Leila, in a beautiful *ksour* in the southern Tunisian desert.

Leila loved to dress up in fine clothes and spent hours in front of the mirror admiring herself. She was always wearing her beautiful silver jewelry, even in bed!

Larbi was proud of his pretty wife and returned each day with gifts. She thanked him and said what a fine husband he was.

One day Larbi took his wife to the market, and Leila picked out the finest dresses, rugs, and cushions, which Larbi bought for her.

"Oh, how I love you, Larbi," cried Leila, and Larbi was so happy!

Leila was tired from shopping, so they stopped at a cafe. It was a warm day, and Leila wanted to cool off in a bath

"Follow me, sweet wife," said Larbi, as they left the cafe and headed to the water trough in the center of town.

"Bathe here, dear Leila," said Larbi, "while I go and buy some grain for our dinner." Larbi hurried off, while Leila slipped into the cool waters of the trough. She swam with her clothes and jewelry on since she was afraid they might be stolen if she took them off.

She cooled off and wanted to climb out, but she couldn't, because her heavy clothes and jewelry weighed her down. She tried to lift herself out of the water but couldn't, so she called for help.

A rooster was pasing by and heard Leila's cries. He ran to the trough and held out his feathers so that she could grasp them and haul herself up.

"I can't grab your feathers!" cried Leila, "They'll rip my fine veils." The rooster held out his foot. "No," said Leila anxiously, "Your claws will rip my dress."

A frog went over and opened his mouth so that he could grasp Leila by the head. "Oh no, Mr. Frog," cried Leila angrily, "You'll pull off my earrings!"

The toad asked for Leila's tail, but she refused, saying he would mar it. "I can't save you if I can't touch you!" he cried.

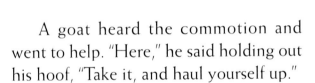

A goat heard the commotion and went to help. "Here," he said holding out his hoof, "Take it, and haul yourself up."

"What? And damage my beautiful gown with your rough and sharp wool? Never!" cried Leila. "Just call my husband."

The animals called Larbi. When he learned his wife was drowning, he ran to the trough. He pulled Leila out and laid her on the ground. Alas, it was too late.

"I could have saved her, but she was afraid my feathers would rip her fine veils," said the rooster.

"I could have helped her, but she said I'd pull off her earrings or mar her tail," said the frog.

"I could have pulled her out, but she said my wool was too rough and my hooves too sharp," said the goat.

"Oh misery!" cried Larbi. "Leila valued her things more than her life. And now she is dead! I am the saddest mouse in the whole world." He turned and slowly walked home sadly.

THE SAHARA FESTIVAL

The Sahara Festival takes place in the town of Douz in central Tunisia, on the edge of the desert. At the end of December thousands of people gather for a celebration of traditional Bedouin life.

Many desert nomads, or Bedouins, live in the region around Douz. They drive flocks of goats, sheep, and camels in search of pasture and desert oases.

The Sahara Festival remembers the traditional lifestyles of the Bedouins and celebrates their culture.

More than 50,000 people gather in Douz for the festival in December. Tunisians, nomads, and tourists mingle while enjoying the festivities.

The camel races are the most exciting. The animals and their riders line up, then the signal sounds, and away they go, kicking lots of sand behind them. The experienced riders make the camels run very fast, while riders who aren't very good may not be able to make the animal move!

Saluki races also take place during the Festival. The saluki is a desert hound that resembles a greyhound and is tall and slim, with very fast legs. The festival is also a time to see how salukis are used to hunt small animals in the desert, which is one way the Bedouins hunt.

The Sahara Festival lasts for a week, but the first day is the best, since there are musical bands that parade in the streets.

Another highlight is the dance performed by Sufis. Sufis practice a religion called Sufism, which teaches love and tolerance of one's neighbors. Sufi dancing consists of dancers who twirl with their arms outstretched.

The medina is filled with shops selling rugs, paintings, pottery, and arts and crafts. In the evenings

Lagmi is a drink enjoyed during the festival, served in a cup like this.

concerts and folkdances are held around campfires. There is also a beauty pageant for Miss Oasis.

Visitors may witness Bedouin weddings that take place during the celebrations.

The festival takes place around the time of the date harvest. People eat fresh dates or drink some *lagmi*, which is a sweet drink made from fermented dates.

There are many stalls set up during the Sahara Festival selling decorated pots.

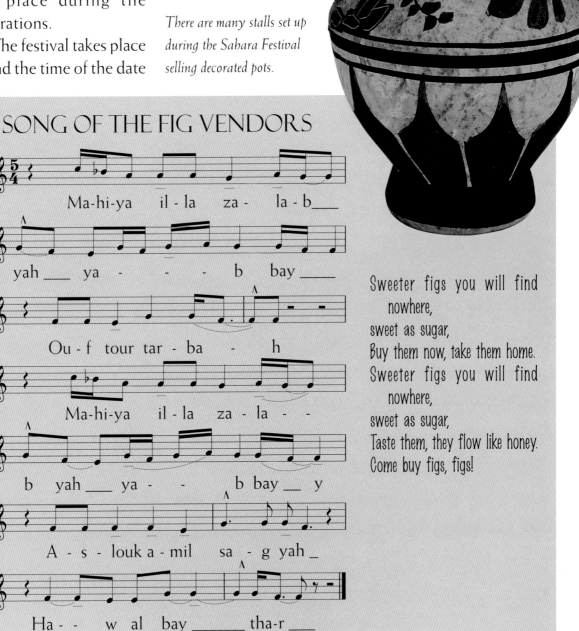

SONG OF THE FIG VENDORS

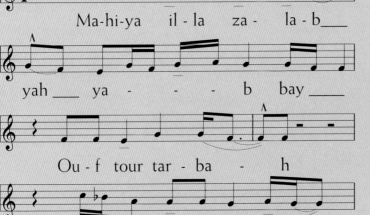

Ma-hi-ya il - la za - la - b___
yah ___ ya - - b bay ____
Ou - f tour tar - ba - h
Ma-hi-ya il - la za - la - -
b yah ___ ya - - b bay __ y
A - s - louk a - mil sa - g yah _
Ha - - w al bay _____ tha-r ___

Sweeter figs you will find
  nowhere,
sweet as sugar,
Buy them now, take them home.
Sweeter figs you will find
  nowhere,
sweet as sugar,
Taste them, they flow like honey.
Come buy figs, figs!

A Berber Wedding

The Berbers are the original non-Arab inhabitants of Tunisia. They have colorful customs and traditions, none more so than traditional Berber weddings.

The Hand of Fatimah (above) is a traditional Berber jewelry design.

Arranged marriages commonly take place in Berber communities. The parents select the life partners for their sons and daughters.

Preparation for the wedding takes months. The parents of the couple meet to plan the wedding. Sometimes the bride and groom may not see each other until the wedding.

Most weddings take place in July and August. The marriage celebrations last as long as three weeks. Separate parties for men and women are held before the wedding.

As the wedding day approaches, the bride is treated specially by her family and friends. They give her presents and decorate her feet and hands with henna, a red dye made from a plant. These designs are very intricate, with swirls and circular patterns. The older relatives of the bride teach her how to be a good wife and mother.

On the wedding day the groom is allowed to be near his wife. The couple are placed on elaborately decorated chairs that resemble thrones. The bride and groom are king and queen for the time of their wedding.

The bride wears a beautiful and heavy dress made with lots of silver jewelry. She also wears a veil covered with silver. Her beautifully decorated hands and feet are the only parts of her body that can be seen.

There is much music, dancing, and laughter, as parents, relatives, friends, and guests sit around the couple eating, drinking, and celebrating this happy occasion.

Berber brides usually wear lots of silver jewelry.

PAINTING HENNA DESIGNS

Henna is a dark-reddish dye that comes from the henna plant. Berber women have been using henna to paint tattoos on their hands and feet for centuries. Patterns include designs that represent flowers, plants, hands, and eyes. The use of henna tattoos is believed to ward away evil spirits and protect and bless the wearer. Berber women are heavily tattooed during their wedding ceremonies.

YOU WILL NEED

A marker with a reddish-brown colored ink
White gloves
A clear sheet of paper
A pencil or pen
Do not use real henna since it takes many weeks to wash out.

1 Soak the gloves in a bowl of tea for a while so they have a flesh-colored tone. Let them dry.

2 Choose a design that you want to draw on your hands. Create one of your own, or flip through design books in libraries.

3 Once you have picked a design, practice it on a clear piece of paper first.

4 When you are comfortable with drawing the pattern, start drawing on the gloves.

5 The marker we used is the color of henna dye; but if you want to make your design more colorful, use other colored markers.

6 Put on the gloves for beautifully designed henna tattoos!

CARTHAGE FESTIVAL

Now a quiet suburb of Tunis, Carthage is one of the oldest and most famous cities in Tunisia. Each July and August the Carthage Festival celebrates the history of the city and the rich heritage of Tunisia in general.

Local legend says that Carthage was founded by the wit and intelligence of a Phoenician queen, Elissa, also called Dido.

Dido set sail from her kingdom, crossed the Mediterranean Sea with her followers, and landed on the coasts of northern Tunisia. There the local prince agreed to grant her as much land as could be contained within an ox hide. Dido cut the hide into very long and thin strips, joined them together, and used the long rope to encircle enough land on which to build the city of Carthage.

The people of ancient Carthage, known today as the Carthaginians, built beautiful palaces, gardens, baths, and temples. The Romans, who conquered the Carthaginians in A.D. 146, built Roman temples, gardens, amphitheaters, and villas in the city.

The ruins of many of these buildings can still be seen preserved in Carthage today. Some of them have also been restored. Many performances during the Carthage Festival are given at these restored Roman buildings.

The festival takes place in July or August. It is an international festival and attracts musical and cultural groups and tourists from around the world.

The performances are held at the restored Roman theater, Hadrian's Theater,

The most popular architectural sights of the Roman era were Roman columns.

originally built in the second century.

Lighting systems, speakers, and machinery

have been added to the ancient structure to make it suitable for cultural performances. Some of the original Roman seats can still be seen.

The festival runs for more than a month, and cultural performances are held at the theater almost every night. Performances are a mixture of traditional and modern dance, music, and theater. The festival is a good opportunity to see many traditional Tunisian dances, including the famous *sharbia*, or pot dance. This dance is often performed at weddings and parties.

The female dancers make swift hip movements as they carry a pot on their shoulders

or on their heads. Their costumes are beautiful, covered in heavy gold and silver ornaments.

During the day visitors wander around the Roman ruins that surround the theater, including the baths of Anthonine, which were once the largest Roman baths in North Africa.

The ruins of ancient Roman homes can also be seen at these sites. Beautiful mosaic tiles exist in some of them. As you watch the Carthage Festival, you realize that Tunisia is a wonderful blend of modern and ancient culture.

This statue is of a woman doing the sharbia, a traditional pot dance in Tunisia.

Music is a very important part of the festival, and some visitors buy music boxes that play traditional tunes.

25

"HANNIBAL IS COMING!"

Although Hannibal was a real-life general of Carthage, some of his achievements seem so amazing that he has become a legendary character. He led his army of elephants over the snowy mountains of the Italian Alps to attack mighty Rome!

HANNIBAL was born in southern Spain when it was under the rule of Carthage. Hannibal's family was of noble blood. Indeed, Hannibal's father, Hamilcar, was a famous general who became the ruler of Carthage.

At the time of Hannibal's birth Carthage was at war with Rome. Both cities were expanding their power over the Mediterranean Sea and the lands that bordered it. Between 264 B.C. and A.D. 146 Rome and Carthage fought a series of three wars known as the Punic Wars. Hannibal is remembered for his achievements in the Second Punic War.

Hannibal became ruler of Carthage when he was twenty-five years old. He was a wise soldier who commanded the respect of his men. He was also very educated and spoke four languages.

Hannibal decided that he would bring the war to Rome's doorstep by invading Rome itself. This had never been done before and required a lot of planning.

But Hannibal was a clever general. Gathering a mighty army of men and African war elephants, he marched north from Spain into France and then into Italy, crossing the mighty Alps on the way.

This image of Hannibal leading his men and elephants through the snowy heights of the Alps is what makes Hannibal such a legendary character. Few people would have thought that elephants could survive such a journey, but they did. Along the way to Rome Hannibal defeated several Roman armies. He was very near Rome when he got the message that Carthage was being attacked by neighboring princes, so he had to return to Carthage. But he was very close to attacking great Rome, and the people of Rome did fear him and his elephants.

For many years after Hannibal's legendary journey to Rome Roman mothers would threaten naughty children by saying, "Hannibal is coming!" This was enough to make any child scared. Roman

historians also record Hannibal's achievements in their books, and Roman generals admired him for his bravery.

Hannibal was eventually defeated by a Roman general, and Carthage was surrendered. He was forced into exile and died at the age of sixty-five.

Although Hannibal was a famous hero, it is only recently that Tunisians have learned about his achievements. As archaeological diggings unearth more ancient ruins, Tunisians are becoming aware of their long and rich history, as well as the legend of Hannibal.

MAKE A MOSAIC OF SEA CREATURES

Mosaics are pictures made of small, colorful squares of stone, marble, or glass. The mosaics found in Tunisia were created on the floors, walls, and ceilings of buildings such as public baths and homes in the Roman cities of Carthage and Dougga. Many Tunisian mosaics show fish and water themes, and reflect the fact that Roman Tunisia relied heavily on sea trade.

YOU WILL NEED

A pair of scissors
Colored foil paper in gold, red, silver, green, blue, and brown
A large sheet of square paper, about 18 inches by 24 inches
Large pictures of fish and other sea creatures such as shrimp, eels, shells, sea horses, and octopuses.
Tracing paper
Glue

1 Trace the pictures of the sea creatures onto the tracing paper. Make sure you have traced all the details, including the scales, lines, eyes, and details on the fins. Make sure each creature is about 10 inches long and quite large.

2 Cut out the sea creatures, and paste them onto the large sheets of square paper.

3 Draw lines on the back of the colored foil 1 inch apart down the entire length. Turn the foil sideways, and do the same lengthwise.

4 Make sure you have covered the foil with even squares.

traced. Leave a small gap in between each mosaic, as well as above and below it. See the closeup to the left.

8 When you have finished with the animals, fill up the remaining space on the paper with blue mosaics to show the ocean.

5 Cut all the colored foil along the lines that you have drawn. You then should have many square pieces of colored foil, or mosaics.

6 Start pasting the mosaic squares onto the animals on the paper.

7 Make sure you paste the mosaics following the lines that you have

FESTIVAL OF FALCONRY

Tunisia is home to many species of birds. Each June in the town of El Haouaria at the tip of the Cap Bon Peninsula in northern Tunisia, there is a falconry festival that celebrates the ancient sport of hunting with peregrine falcons, a bird of prey.

Falcons are large birds of prey with sharp claws, or talons, and hooked beaks. In the past they have been used for hunting other birds, such as partridge and quail.

The falcons fly to the Cap Bon Peninsula on their way north to Sicily, an island in the Mediterranean. They lay eggs early in the year, and young falcons appear in March and April. During this time Tunisian falconers, people who train falcons to hunt, capture these birds, as well as kestrels, another bird of prey.

The falconers train their birds to catch smaller birds and prepare them for the Festival of Falconry in June. Many townsfolk are falconers and keep their birds in their homes. It is an amazing sight to see dozens of these birds swoop down and capture their prey before returning to their falconers to perch on their arms. Because their talons are so sharp, the falconers have to cover their arms with leather gloves so that they will not be cut when the birds perch on their arms. The festival is very popular with tourists and Tunisians alike.

WORDS TO KNOW

Amphitheater: An oval or round building with multi-leveled seats around a central open area.

Congested: To fill to excess; overcrowded or overburdened.

Endangered: Being at the risk of disappearing completely or no longer being in existence.

Enormous: Huge.

Entrails: The inner organs of the body.

Folklore: The traditional beliefs or customs of a people.

Incense: An aromatic substance producing a sweet smell when burned.

Inhabit: To live or dwell in a place, as people or animals.

Intricate: Having many interrelated parts or facets; entangled or involved.

Miraculous: Performed by or involving a supernatural power.

Nomad: Someone who has no permanent place of living, but moves from place to place in search of food or a place to live.

Obedience: The state of complying with or being submissive to authority.

Pamper: To treat with excessive or extreme indulgences, kindness, or care.

Prophet: A person who speaks for God or a deity, or to some religious purpose.

Sacred: Devoted or dedicated to a deity or to some religious purpose.

Swoop: To sweep down through the air.

Tapestries: A fabric on which colored threads are woven by hand to produce a reversible design.

ACKNOWLEDGMENTS

WITH THANKS TO:
Monia Ben-Khaled and Besma Ben-Hassine for all their hard work in obtaining the lyrics and tune of Ellila Eid.

PHOTOGRAPHS BY:
Haga Library Japan (cover), Sam Yeo (p. 10 top, p. 12 botom, p. 13, p. 16 left, p. 17), ANA Press Agency (p. 22 top), Yu Hui Ying (all other images)

ILLUSTRATIONS BY:
Enrico Sallustio (p. 1, p. 4, p. 7), Lee Kowling (p. 19, p. 27) and Cake (p. 5, p. 30).

SET CONTENTS